Tea in the Pacific Northwest

Tea in the Pacific Northwest

Poems by

Jim Landwehr

© 2024 Jim Landwehr. All rights reserved.
This material may not be reproduced in any form, published,
reprinted, recorded, performed, broadcast,
rewritten or redistributed without
the explicit permission of Jim Landwehr.
All such actions are strictly prohibited by law.

Cover design by Shay Culligan
Cover image by Walter Jack Savage
Author photo by Sarah Jessica Landwehr

ISBN: 978-1-63980-515-0

Kelsay Books
502 South 1040 East, A-119
American Fork, Utah 84003
Kelsaybooks.com

This collection is dedicated to the Wisconsin Fellowship of Poets. Their community, support, and encouragement sustain my writing.

Acknowledgments

While this book is comprised of my words, it could not have happened without the support of my writing colleagues, past and present. My love for poetry goes back as far as my eighth grade English class where we were asked to dissect and critique a poem and present it to class. Mr. Gallett's words of encouragement about that critique stuck with me for life.

From there, it was the genius of people like Richard Brautigan, Mary Oliver, Billy Collins, and dozens of local Wisconsin poets that spurred me to begin writing my own. My poetic pursuits continue to make me a better writer in all genres.

As always, thank you to my wife, Donna and my kids Sarah and Benjamin, for their continual support and encouragement in all my writing endeavors. Thank you to all my readers who have ever told me that you enjoyed my work. It means the world to me, as it does to any author/poet.

I'd be remiss not to thank Karen Davies, Delisa Hargrove, and the rest of the staff at Kelsay Books for believing in my work and bringing this book to the world. Their professionalism, attention to detail, and follow through are second to none. The beautiful cover image is the product of artist, writer, and friend, Walter Jack Savage, a fellow displaced Minnesotan who positively bleeds artistic and literary talent.

And, finally, thank you to the magazines and journals below that published some of the poems found in this collection.

Blue Heron Review: "Winchester County"

Grey Thoughts: The Writers Club: "Huntington Beach"

A Line Meant: "Art Attack"

Moss Piglet: "Dress Blues," "1970 Datsun," "Bake at 350," "Tea in the Pacific Northwest," "Suitable for Framing," "My Posthumous Dialog," "Rule Breakers," "Minnesota Boys," "By Pedal," "Each a Breed of Their Own," "2050 Anticipated Trends," "Photo Retention"

The Orchards Poetry Journal: "Wordnapped"

Poetry is Dead: "Valley of the Dead"

Syncopation Journal: "Rock and Roll Can Never Die"

Unwashed Zine: "Who I Am"

The Waterwheel Review and *Wisconsin People and Ideas:* "It Is, It's Not"

Wisconsin Fellowship of Poets Calendar: "Notes from the Edges"

Wreath of Golden Laurels Anthology: "Amusement"

Contents

Sadness	13
Dress Blues	14
Huntington Beach, 1983	15
The Meeting	16
1970 Datsun	17
Confessions of an Ambivert	19
Return Flight	20
Winchester County	21
Heartographer	22
Nostalgia	23
Lockdown Levity	24
Bake at 350	26
Three Haikus Not Yet Banned	27
Monochromatic	28
First Impressions	29
The Conference	30
Resistive Reflectivity	31
Tea in the Pacific Northwest	32
Bat Day at the Met	33
The Four Walls of Me	34
Suitable for Framing	36
Free Falling	37
Trout Fishing in the Driftless Area	38
The Kick	39
The Collision of Philosophy and Poetry	41
House Arrest Haikus	42
Wordnapped	43
My Posthumous Dialog	44
The Church of St. Vincent	45
The Pink Lady	46
Valley of the Dead	47
It Is, It's Not	48

Amusement	49
Named	50
Notes from a Part-Time Buddhist Hack	53
Pickup Ball	55
Breathgiving	57
Hobby and Hoarding Both Start With H	58
Rule Breakers	59
It Feels/It Felt	60
Please Hold for a Limerick	61
A Shell of Ourselves	62
Peace by Piece	63
Notes from the Edges	64
Divided Together	65
Rock and Roll Can Never Die	66
Art Attack	67
By Pedal	68
Who I Am	69
The Book of Her	70
Each a Breed of Their Own	72
Funeral Wish	74
2050 Anticipated Trends	75
Haikus for the Loner	77
Minnesota Boys	78
Losing Arguments	79
Superior Sister	80
Photo Retention	81

Sadness

She carried her sadness in a
flamingo print bag
hanging like a gallows of sorrow
from her delicate shoulder.
Inside the bag
the sadness lay
between the ChapStick
and the false promises
of her pocketbook
home to four lonely dollar bills
folded morosely against one another
doing their best to cheer her
but ultimately only serving to
worsen her condition.
If things didn't get rosier soon
she would need a bigger satchel
perhaps an upgrade to an
albatross sack
with enough room
for a lifetime of grief.
Friends told her she should dump
her sadness into the Susquehanna River
but she wasn't sure she was ready
to let go of it altogether
she liked to take it out once in a while
and wear it like a burka of distress
revealing only her mournful eyes
because without her sadness
she might be tempted to savor
joy, happiness, and contentment.
So she kept it nestled
in a bag she carried
to use on occasion
like a flamethrower of hopelessness.

Dress Blues

It was difficult to tell
which was more uncomfortable
my lanky, seventeen-year-old self
posing for an Instamatic photo
or the powder blue tuxedo I wore
to my senior year formal dance.

The tux was a deeply discounted
limited-time offer
from Robert's Rent-a-Tux
where I'd saved myself twenty dollars
at the expense of any semblance
of style, comfort, or cool.

It was a fashion mashup
between a '70s pimp and a Smurf;
a collaborative work tailored
by Willie Wonka and Austin Powers
and while Elvis had Blue Suede Shoes
here I was wearing the rest of it.

Blue bowtie, blue tinted ruffles
blue vest, blue jacket
blue pants, blue trim
blue buttons, blue socks
a budding Blue-Collar Man
all Tangled Up in Blue.

Huntington Beach, 1983

It took me twenty-two years
two thousand miles
fistfuls of No Doz
twelve rest stops
a sleepless Colorado night
and forty hours in a rental car
to finally see the Pacific.
Suddenly, there it was
stretched before me
rendered in its finest
California spandex
with leather waves
crashing like Morrison
at the Alta Cienega hotel
in a drunken crescendo
of whiskey and flotsam,
a song without lyrics.
In my youth I needed
to see and touch it,
taste its salty brine
submit to its power
its unseen tidal force
as I cast myself into
the softness of its hold
bodysurfing my way
out of my midwestern
naiveté towards the depravity
false promises and
distant broken dreams
of Los Angeles.

The Meeting

Everyone around the table was
navigating through the meeting
casting noncommitments around freely
evading work with vagueness and excuses
nodding to the boss with their
personal variations of the boss nod.
The meeting was a formulaic soul killer
serving no measurable purpose
except to do what meetings do best
which is generate more meetings.
Attendees took notes at times
but those who wished they
weren't there in that meeting
did not take a single note.
I did not take notes.
The meeting dragged on and on
its leader,
clearly new to leading meetings,
stopped caring himself halfway through.
I actually saw his spirit leave his body
as it yawned itself toward the ceiling.
And once everyone had their shot
at dropping a few buzzwords
and trite acronyms like bad fiction
leveraging the platform
empowering the 'A' team
using synergy to increase market share
while ensuring ROI for Q3 on the R2D2
they eventually called the meeting done
in part at the realization that
it could have been an email, but
mostly because it had become
that wet log you try to burn
in your campfire
but it just won't start.

1970 Datsun

In the late seventies
a friend of mine owned a red Datsun.
Well, it was red when it was new
but by the time he inherited it
the paint had faded to
a reluctant shadow of itself.
It looked like it had been touched up
using broken crayon remnants
in distant shades of red
from a box of 64 Crayolas
with a built-in sharpener.
The car was slowly being disassembled
by rust and the cavernous potholes
of all those Minnesota winters
pounding on it like a drunk uncle.
Salt had eaten away the floorboards
and slowly spit them on the pavement
of the highways and byways
so that from the front seat
one could watch the road whiz by
giving the car a Flintstone feel.
The front driver's side fender rusted,
and eventually expelled itself
from the body altogether.
It had had enough of this heap.
This left the springs and shocks exposed
to the winter elements and St. Paul's rain.
They resented the fender for defecting
and leaving them with the pitiful owner
and no roof over their head.

The red Datsun had the engine
of a steadfast, reliant friend
like a dog who can cook and clean
but its body treated my friend
like that girlfriend his
mama told him not to date.
They eventually broke up.

Confessions of an Ambivert

I get drunk on people
but they give me the worst
hangovers.

The people drag me out
past ten o'clock sometimes
talking.

Me and them, we get along
like old friends talking, laughing and
reminiscing.

They finally say their goodbyes
let's do this again soon
pleading.

They're also part of my recovery stage
solitude, quiet, maybe some water
rehashing.

I love the people and am one of them
but my inner introvert hates them
demanding.

Return Flight

The deconstruction of his heart
happened on the tarmac
in a cramped seat next to
a window etched by miles.
His was a goodbye wrapped
in sorrow and a destitution
of his soul,
an emotional emptiness
that clanged leaden in his chest.
The spaces where her words
once touched his own
on the lips
were like parchment in
the valley of his despondency.
So his anguish rode with him on
a flight to a destination
devoid of meaning, significance
and color,
but mostly
of her.

Winchester County

Outside the warmth of the cabin
I stand under the heavens
smoking a cigarette
neck craned skyward
while drags of nicotine
accompanied by the
multitude of distant stars
that make up the Milky Way
combine to lift me,
my thoughts
my past and my future
to a place of refuge,
peace and gratefulness.

As a self-proclaimed
once-a-year smoker
each drag seems to help
with my struggle
to make sense of the
busyness and distraction
back home in my desert
of concrete, asphalt and steel.

For me it is a reckoning,
a fleeting moment of
sanctuary and contentment
conjured among the Jack Pines
and the watch of the moon
but also among the lost moments
spent long ago
worrying about tomorrow.

Heartographer

The map to the center of his heart
was drawn with measured hand
and featured twisty roads
with names like Sorrow Street
Struggler's Way and Burden Lane.
They were roads and byways
that paved the course to the villages
of Love's Fade and Isolation's Keep,
places filled with uncertainty
bordering emergent meadows,
those green pastures of promise
cut by rivers flowing with dreams.
The map was torn and taped
tattered at the edges
from the twists and turns
of a disoriented and lost traveler
but the map held its place in his life
as the guide leading him back home.

Nostalgia

Some long for a time that
probably never was
a place that exists more
in their mind than it
ever did in reality
a rosier present than
the current state of affairs
an embellished set of
memories and circumstances
that sometimes prohibit them
from appreciating today
and you can sloganize it
with a curt saying like
In the good old days
but slogans are hollow
promises of something
that looks like a Cadillac
but handles like a golf cart
missing a wheel.

Lockdown Levity

It is day thirleventy-forty-nine
of the godawful quarantine
and working from home
my dog welcomes our
constant unwavering presence
while my cat is grumbling
about getting her own place.

The thought of taking a vacation
to a cabin in the driftless area
was kicked around by my wife
until she realized that getting a
place to stay with me where
nothing is open or accessible
would be a whole lot like staying home.

As part of my attempt to get out
and stay in decent physical shape
I walk before and after work every day
it is my time to reflect and enjoy nature
but the route has become tiresome
and after nine weeks of it
I know exactly where *every* dog lives.

It is the third Wednesday of this week
and my wife and I want a redo of April
the lost month of what just happened?
May screams by happy to be history
ushering in the uncertainty of June
August is almost certain to disappoint
and weekends look identical to Tuesday.

Before the godawful quarantine
my wife and I went out for coffee
and conversation every Saturday morning
it was our time to catch up eye to eye
now we order takeout coffee and bakery
that we eat and drink around our table at home
and it positively, absolutely, is not the same.

Bake at 350

Here in Wisconsin people call it casserole
but I am forever endeared to its true name
hotdish!
and it is funny how such a simple,
one might even call it, bohemian
entree
can be considered one of my favorite
culinary memories of growing up in saint paul
minnesota
mom made it with all the standard ingredients
hamburger, macaroni, onion, peppers and tomato
paste
baked at 350 until the top was lightly crusted
it was the best part of an otherwise average Wednesday
night
disrespected as the food of the proletariat
none of us six kids cared what the rich folks
thought
the only upper crust we cared about
was on the bread that accompanied our
hotdish!

Three Haikus Not Yet Banned

some I've read, some not
the book banners rise again
have we learned nothing?

all of the banned books
banished to the ocean floor
means more scuba sales

Light in the Attic
Fahrenheit Four Fifty-One
and I turned out okay

Monochromatic

She stares back at me
though I am not there
and she is not here

Third in line of seven
she was intended for a lifetime
but didn't make it five years

I know she happened
the evidence is irrefutable
it's all in black and white

She seems like a happy kid
smiling big most times
in her little girl dresses

There she is lakeside
a shot by the Christmas tree
another blowing out candles

Then the saddest of all
in a hospital gown
clutching a toy dog

Like a beautiful shadow
of all the rest of us
she gives us these glimpses

This sister I never knew
unlike the rest of us
remains forever young in pictures

First Impressions

It's alleged that our people are
made from cheese and bratwurst
chiseled by hard work and heavy snow
entertained by polka and packers
raised on values and common sense
fans of bucks and badgers
seekers of hodags and musky
festers of summer and oktober
drinkers of beer and a bump.
It is said we are these things
and none can be refuted.

The Conference

I felt like I'd overtaken
the conversation
unintendedly

Butted in and asserted
myself, yeah me
rudely

I didn't back down either
I loved me
wholeheartedly

I'm not usually this way
sometimes, I'm nice
occasionally

Resistive Reflectivity

(A Sijo poem)

When I look, I see my past. My deeds, my faults, my affections
I seek truths across my life, its fits and starts, its do-overs
but I rest, knowing I have done all I came for, it's enough.

Tea in the Pacific Northwest

I had tea with a Sasquatch yesterday
having come across him during a hike
in the cold drizzle of the Pacific Northwest

His hut was deep in the woods far from trail
he took me there because he said I looked cold
his English was better than most of my friends

The tea was a mix of pine needles, moss, and turnip peelings
claims he'd stolen the turnips from a garden in town
said he wasn't proud of it, but what's a tea-loving Bigfoot to do?

I asked him why he and his kind were so elusive
he said it used to be the fear of being shot at
but now it was more a hatred of all the political bickering

In the corner was a tattered copy of Slaughterhouse Five
he asked if the fire-storming of Dresden really happened
when I said yes, I think his eyes watered up a little

When it came time to leave, I invited him to my house
he laughed and laughed, shaking his sagittally-crested head
why leave his simple life for stress of the city?

He made me promise not to tell anyone we'd met
after all, his reputation of being hard-to-find was on the line
so I'll leave it to you to decide if it ever happened

Bat Day at the Met

(Metropolitan Stadium, Bloomington MN, 1973)

Our one day at the ballpark every summer
was courtesy of our grandma
to say she was a baseball fanatic
only serves to cheapen the adjective

On Bat Day one year she took 3 of us
seated in the upper grandstand
37 stories above a field of green
the bases looked like Chiclets

By the third inning boredom set in
when our attention turned concessionary
because while we liked baseball
a boy's stomach only holds 2 good innings

37 stories up, it's a different game
pop flies look bound for the stars
a ball looks like a strike and vice versa
but the ice cream vendor stands tall

Five innings into a pitching duel
thousands of other bored kids
pounded their souvenir bats on the risers
creating juvenile thunder for the home team

I remember grandma scored the games
writing Mandarin symbols in the program
a shorthand account of Bat Day history
penned so she could relive what she missed

The Four Walls of Me

(Thoughts on pandemic solitude)

I always thought seclusion during a pandemic like this would be a dream come true. The first three weeks were dreamy. Now I just need to have coffee with someone other than my wife.

Some people might use this time in isolation to write a novel. I choose to despair writing pandemic poetry and drinking rye whiskey.

My wife started us drinking rye whiskey after bingeing on the Outlander series on Netflix. It seems plagues are also good for developing bad habits.

I wear a mask when I leave my isolation to shop or get gas. The right-wing conspiracy folks give me looks of pity and disdain. I think to myself, I'm just here to get fruit without killing your grandmother.

My dreams during this time of lockdown have been both bizarre and realistic. However, none of them are as bizarre or realistic as my waking hours these past two months.

I've had five different pieces accepted for publication this past week. It seems plagues are good fertilizer for my literary muse, but bad for people.

I take walks every morning before working from home. The streets are eerily quiet and it feels like I am the only person on earth. The fenced-in dogs along my path jolt me back to reality.

Every Saturday, my wife and I get takeout coffee and bakery from the coffee shop we used to frequent before COVID-19 was a thing. We sit at our kitchen table and talk, but it's not the same.

People ask what I am doing with all this new free time? I remind them that I still work 40 hours a week, making my free time the same as before the pandemic, only lonelier.

I Zoom and Skype and Google Meet with friends and coworkers. I've developed an intermittent speech delay and a bad habit of talking over people.

When people want to get together in a "socially distant" location, I interrogate them as though I was going to sleep with them. *Who have you been with recently? Who were they with? How long were you together? Did you touch them?*

I've learned to accept disappointment. I canceled all my trips for the next 6 months because even if I did go, it wouldn't be the same. It's easier to be sad than hopeful.

To be completely truthful, one positive that has come out of the pandemic is the ability to say no to just about everything, without guilt. A small part of me loves that.

When I go fishing alone in my kayak, it is almost like there is no pandemic at all. The great plague of 2020 comes rushing back when I get to the launch and have to negotiate distancing from the people just launching.

While I long for lost vacations and the feel of normalcy, it is glaringly apparent that the thing I miss most is the presence of my kids and their freedom to visit at a moment's notice. Pandemics make the heart grow fonder.

Suitable for Framing

On vacation visiting family,
I took a morning walk
at a nearby nature preserve
to clear the mind, stretch the legs
and rehash conversations
I'd had with people.
Half an hour into it
a craggy, majestic oak
yelled at me so loud
it stopped me in my tracks.
It stood there preaching to the sky
or maybe it was worshipping
the same sun I was that day
its branches stripped bare by winter
fully extended upward exulting
shouting in the language of all oaks
hey human, take my picture!
So I obliged, in part because
the tree was big and imposing
but more because its figure and form
pasted against the backdrop of clouds
was worthy of, and demanded
complete adoration and respect.
It stood there stiff as a board
posed with fingers outstretched
pointing the way to everywhere
while I snapped a couple shots
giving the stately oak the promise
of eternal life in a poem I once wrote.

Free Falling

It is easy to look back and say it was all good
knowing of course, none of it was easy
the emotional bumps and bruises we took
walking the twisted path of life's labyrinth

When a poet hits a certain point in life
everything takes on measure
their childhood is scrutinized for all it was
and everything else relates back to that

Their teen years tumbling through high school
reaching for the branch of friendship while
crashing down mountainsides of loneliness
wondering who waits at the bottom

College and jobs both take them places
putting their nose to the grindstone
for forty years of indentured gratitude
working to live, living to work

Mixed in may be partners and kids; or not.
a person always leaves a wake behind
of people they loved and who loved them back
until one or the other grew up or moved on

Eventually old age plays its part in all of it
to remind them that inevitably the show ends
as they run to catch up to what they've missed
thinking someday will be better than the present

But if they look at the transactions
the good times serving as deposits
and hard times as the debt collector calling
the ledger always balances in the black

Trout Fishing in the Driftless Area

The man who never claimed
to be a trout fisherman
tried his luck just to see
if maybe he could smooth talk
a brookie into falling for his ruse.
He'd heard amazing stories about
trout fishing in the Driftless region.
Tales of trout the size of Wildebeests
and as numerous as Subarus
at a farmers market.
So he took a rod and reel that
never claimed to be for trout fishing
and clomped down to the stream.
He arrived just in time for
the black fly rally, streamside.
They buzzed around his meaty head
wearing tiny black leather jackets.
He moved down the stream
casting and swatting until
he felt the tug of a trout so bored
even a feathered spinner with hooks
looked interesting enough to
risk its life over,
besides it was lunchtime.
And for just a few moments
the man who never claimed
to be a trout fisherman
was one.

The Kick

He is eleven years old standing six yards deep
standing nervously with empty hands extended
awaiting the snap from center
as punter for his intramural team
he can see exactly where he wants to put the ball.
What he cannot see from six yards deep
is a single moment of what his future holds
only the crouching center, the ball,
and the distant return man.
He is not yet privy to the cliques
he will fall into in high school.
For the moment he is only an anxious punter
who does not know his major or even which college
but really, really doesn't want his kick blocked.
At the moment, his first job out of college
does not seem important
nor the academic probation
he overcame to graduate.
Only the kick does. This kick.
Later, when he moves to out of state
to take a new job
there will be no thought given to that day as a punter
only to the job.
That new job.
He wipes his hands on his football pants
and listens as the signal caller begins signaling
Down. Set . . .
Marriage and parenthood seem more distant
than the opponent's return man standing on the forty
and at the moment, he is only focused on the latter.

When his kids graduate and move away
and retirement looms in his near future
the details on how far he kicked will have faded
and much like the rest of his life
he will only remember he did the best he could.
The center snaps the ball to his waiting hands.

The Collision of Philosophy and Poetry

Routine is comfort
disguised as order
needed by those
who fear change

Habits make us do
things we once thought
necessary or appealing but
now they just make us

Our points of view
vary from place to place
not the same yesterday
as tomorrow or last year

Vices are the disharmony
between the love of self
the need for personal justice
and our core selfishness

Our emotional outbursts
spring from karmic energy
welled up in our souls
erupting to release us

Inner peace overcomes
when it merges today's joy
with recognition of our mortality
freeing self from selfish

House Arrest Haikus

Zooming taught me skills
I speak with virtual lag
overtalking too

COVID has turned days
into two separable
parts coffee and beer

One hundred twenty
each day very much like the
one we just got through

Wordnapped

he kidnapped words and held them
hostage with a steep ransom
kept them tied up
hidden
closeted

he tried to make the words talk
to fess up to their true meaning
or reveal their intent
disclose
divulge

he bribed them with chocolate,
coffee, pastries, even whiskey
hoping to brainwash them
erase
rewrite

but the words were a stubborn lot
they knew their true worth
was beyond his talents
silence
blocked

so he increased his demands
threatened the true owner of the words
gave them one last chance
final
ultimatum

while he was eating jelly toast
the words escaped his entrapment
and ran like hell
forever
lost

My Posthumous Dialog

I wish you could have
lived to see your grandkids grow
they have your features

You never should have
walked into that bar that night
it was your last drink

As fate would have it
these words have gone unheeded
cast up to heaven

I wish I could have
told you how much I love you
with my last few breaths

I never should have
walked into that bar that night
of that you are right

My life of would haves
was spent looking down on you
wishing we could have

The Church of St. Vincent

When I first moved to Wisconsin
I had trouble understanding
the Packer religion
and all its attendant mythology
stories of the greats
Starr, Hornung, and Davis
giants of an age ago.
Having migrated from the land
of the Purple Gang
we had our own folklore
Tark, Foreman and Page.
Then, when Majkowski pulled us
from the depths of football misery
and turned the reigns over to
Favre, White, and Freeman
who won us a Super Bowl
something I'd never seen before
it was a coming to faith.
#GoPackGo

The Pink Lady

My grandmother owned a Model A
she'd had it restored and painted pink
then named it the Pink Lady
I cannot make this stuff up

She usually gave us grandkids
one ride a year in the middle of summer
pulled up to our house and ooogah!
out we'd scramble for the rumble seat

I remember the dieseling of her engine
underpowered and subtle in its glory
a three-on-the tree was all she had
topping out at 47 downhill with a tailwind

Grandma in her scarf and overcoat
once took us on the freeway
waving to everyone who passed
some honking, some waving, others "birding"

She was the queen of St. Paul, I suppose
riding in her royal pink carriage
waving her Queen Elizabeth wave
to the bourgeoisie in their Impalas

Valley of the Dead

I'd heard enough about their shows
throngs of followers tracking them
as they crossed the country
three-hour jams complete with intermissions
freaks, vagabonds, and rusted-out hippies
so decided I needed to find out for myself
a music lover who knew many of their songs
grateful they were playing Alpine Valley
on a warm Saturday in June, 1987
a friend and I showed up high
because it was mandatory
only to find the parking lot
was its own beautiful freakshow
vans, tents, and other paraphernalia
in a flashback to the sixties
clearly this wasn't just any concert
and when the music started
everyone rose to their feet dancing
in a huge, swaying, pulsing,
smoking display of humanity
breathing nothing but peace and love
living in only that very moment
all of it punctuated
by the naked stoner guy
doing no harm to anyone
but chased by security
whose number one occupation
was shielding women
from his nakedness

It Is, It's Not

It's still a ways away. It's going to go away, you know. It's still there. It is, or it isn't. It's in the mail. It's in the console. It's the perfect fit. It's me versus you. It's something we can all look back to. It's forward looking. It's around here somewhere. It's the American Dream. It's far from my reach. It's only six weeks until raise time. It's not guaranteed. It's destined for nowhere. It's written in Sanskrit. It's translated to mean something unknown. It's in the works. It's not in the cards. It's on my dresser. It's not that. It's not the way that goes. It's not their best work. It's not that funny, is it? It's not Fleetwood Mac. It's not nice to be right all the time. It's not nice to boast. It's not a miracle to me. It's not pure. It's not the worst thing that could happen. It's not who you think it is. It's not over there, I said. It's not impossible to go back to school at your age. It's not that far on the map. It's not something you could actually get a job doing. It's none of your business. It's not my first rodeo. It's not too bad going down. It's third and long at the Rams' 38-yard line. It's all a big money thing. It's guaranteed 2-day delivery. It's neither of yours now, goddammit! It is to be read along with my will. It's such a waste of time. It's at least something. It's over there, I said! It's neither the best, nor the worst. It's nothing compared to yours. It's snowing! It's time to go potty, Dog. It's hell getting old. It's cold in here. It's not cold in here! It's not on this map anywhere. It's not yours. It's impossible to hear in this room. It's winding down. It's incomprehensible to me. It's poetry wearing winter camouflage. It's getting late. It's not like this could go on forever, could it?

Amusement

We ride them in pursuit of something far
outside our average daily experience
these ten-story death wheels
these perilous whirling vomitoriums
these four-person runaway trains
churning in frenetic pirouettes
without an engineer or pilot in sight
assembled in haste by carnies battling
hangovers from last night's trailer blowout.
We ride them to shake up our routine
put a good scare in us, make us scream
make our heart come up into our throat
grip the safety bar like it means something
through loops and turns at breakneck speed
holding on in hopes that we make it through
this horribly, fantastically terrifying window
of so-called amusement.

Named

Each kid had a name
and a story to tell
now stories untold
because these bullets
lead to nothing
but screams of grief
an ocean of sorrow.

Bullets 1-3 hit Matt
who would have been
a programmer
while 4-6 hit the whiteboard
and 7-12 took
out Kristi, a future
mother
-a great one at that-
if not for those six bullets.

Shots 13-23 were used
to terminate forever the
friendship of Charles, Justin
and Miguel who
were talking about
the coming weekend
just a minute earlier.
a weekend that would pass
without them.

Rounds 24 through 27
were errant shots of mercy
splintering the desktops
of higher learning
once graced by kids
of generations where
assault rifles were
weapons of war
not a means for
violent revenge.

Bullets 28-33
entered Mr. Goldman
killing him for
shielding Na'Quala
a survivor
scarred for life
who would never
emotionally recover.
She's still dying
a different sort
of death.

Bullets 34-86
took from this earth
eleven other
bright lights

Willie
Stephanie
Maria
Tosha
Ben
Mia
Isaiah
Rachel
Ignatious
Celia
Shanequa

and with them went
beautiful smiles
dinner conversations
graduations
birthdays and
weddings never held
goodbyes unsaid
last I love yous, missed.

These children
were taken
from us
by an assaulting
weapon of war
good for
one thing.

Killing dreams.

Notes from a Part-Time Buddhist Hack

Our lives are a breath, whispered
on a mirror
they hang for a few moments
then evaporate

Those holy moments come and go
between friends
sometimes over coffee or beer
other times outdoors

We carry our peace as a witness
if we try
the alternative is carrying ourselves
just making noise

Before time catches us wasting it
on idle pursuits
turn it into something worth remembering
with someone else

It takes twenty seconds to text a child
I love you
or twenty years convincing them if
you never did

I rarely regret a morning walk
all by myself
but I've never regretted a walk taken
with my spouse

Winter is nature's way of telling us
to slow down
summer, however, hollers for itself
get outside now!

College does not signal the end of learning
but begins it
those that quit seeking to better themselves
often times succeed

Music is the balm for many ailments
in your life
dancing lifts the spirit and reminds us to
do it often

Pickup Ball

For me, the baseball spectacle
was not about
perfectly manicured infields
megawatt sound systems
climate controlled domed stadiums
overpriced concessions
and endless pitching changes
interrupted periodically by
ten seconds of action.
For me, baseball
was about pickup games
on an asphalt field
with painted baselines
crushed soda can bases
and a chain-link backstop.
It was about
screaming one-hoppers
hitting the palm of
my garage sale fielder's mitt
like a Nolan Ryan fastball
causing a momentary
localized yard sale
of discarded glove and ball
while I hopped and flapped
that stinging left hand
like it was aflame
as the baserunner rounded first.
It was about
ghost runners
all-time pitchers
and right field automatic outs
for lack of enough players.

For me, it was never about
multimillion dollar contracts
superstar endorsements
and twelve-dollar beers.
It was about
bringing your own bat
sharing your glove
and four fouls is an out.
It was about
kids playing a kids game
purely for the love of it
on a summer day.

Breathgiving

Her voice lilts
over the air
breathy and precise
always on key
soaring to heights
when necessary
descending with grace
to stunning lows
flowing effortlessly
from within her lungs
to meet their fullness
upon the skies
these songs are art
breathed into being
as an offering from
artist to humanity
and from there
lay themselves softly
into the soul
of the man
weeping for reasons
he cannot understand.

Hobby and Hoarding Both Start With H

As a boy, it once was just a hobby
sports cards of his favorite athletes
with the no-names destined for
the spokes of his stingray bike.

After discovering the cardboard heroes
held monetary value as well as intrinsic,
what was just a hobby
became an unhealthy obsession

Instead of individual cards he bought complete sets
a gateway drug to other memorabilia
autographed jerseys, helmets, stadium seats,
bases, bats, gloves, pennants, even infield dirt.

It piled up around his house
collectible detritus collecting dust
protected from oily hands
in plastic sleeves and Tupperware bins

The hobby morphed into hoarding
without his even knowing
until a stack of Sports Illustrateds
fell and crushed his dog Shaq.

Fixated on finding a rare Mickey Mantle
he never realized Shaq was gone
off to dog heaven and extra innings
under the weight of yesterday's sports stars.

Rule Breakers

It was the eccentric ones
those that wrote outside the lines
and broke most of the conventional rules.
They took literature, poetry and art
beat it out of submission with pens and brushes
gave it to their readers and critics
and told them to love-it-or-leave-it
proclaiming, *It's me. It's who I am. It's my ART!*
So it is with reverence when I speak of
Brautigan, Kerouac and Dali
Hunter S. Thompson, Ginsberg and Picasso
the thinkers, the madmen and the drinkers
who created a new paradigm for me
a fledgling writer unafraid
to push the boundaries of
chapter, stanza and verse
to knock around the rules taught in school
and let them know that's not who I am
they are not the boss of me
I'm the writer, the author, the poet
and they are just the words
awaiting rescue from the stifling
restrictions of rules made by
uptight men and women of yesterday.

It Feels/It Felt

It feels like the first time. It felt like a dream within a dream. It feels as though your mind is made up. It felt like going home. It feels like time is speeding past. It felt plastic. It feels like it's gonna rain. It felt unnatural. It feels like you're contradicting your story. It felt that way for a long time. It feels like you're judging me. It felt like the time had come. It feels like it's the size of a walnut. It felt like we were nearing the end. It feels like we should go. It felt like none of this was ever planned on. It feels done. It felt good. It feels like it could use one more stanza. It felt a little too long. If feels like I cannot stop writing. It felt like I needed to say, 'enough!' It feels good we can share what we really think. It felt like déjà vu.

Please Hold for a Limerick

Press one for appointments it said
or three if you'd rather instead
speak to a person who's living
but less than forgiving
or just hold the line till you're dead

A Shell of Ourselves

We are a crew of students
learning to row a sixty-foot shell.
Day after day we work on technique
correcting an unending list of wrongs
outside elbows too low, poor feathering
and a constant, nagging list to port.
The coxswain encourages and corrects
looking to be supportive but firm
as we try and iron out our collective flaws.
Interspersed, there are fleeting moments
of synchronicity, rhythm, and rowing Zen
moments that will bring us all back tomorrow
because despite our faults and miscues
we are in this to get better, together.
So, we do what we came here for
we row.

Peace by Piece

What form does peace take?
Does it come from above
in a fiery, billowing mushroom cloud
and an encore of radioactive fallout?
Or perhaps it comes
floating on an aircraft carrier
wearing a banner
of an accomplished mission?
No.
Nor is it a treaty, an agreement
or an accord.
Peace rarely honors
the paper it is written on
or the politicians who penned it.
Peace is breathed into the hearts
of men and women one
act of loving kindness at a time.
Feed the hungry,
comfort the lonely
house the homeless
forgive the sinner.
Until we have peace among
ourselves we are incapable
of spreading it abroad.

Notes from the Edges

There was a time in my life
where the appeal of living
like indecipherable notes
in the margins of my pages
seemed perfectly okay.
Until then I'd lived life
on the straight and narrow-
ruled whitespace of my
pages largely because that
was what everyone expected.
I have to admit those days
hanging out in the gutters
and fringes of my twenties
almost falling off the page
or ink-blotting into illegibility
were reckless, immature and
entirely necessary chapters
of my unique story.

Divided Together

(A skinny poem)

Milwaukee and its segregation
Together
Separate
Black
White
Together
Brothers
Sisters
Humans
Together
And it's Milwaukee segregation

Rock and Roll Can Never Die

When Ric Ocasek got to heaven
he met up with George Harrison
in a smoky bar on the sketchy side
of the pearly gates

George confessed he struggled
his whole musical career
living in the shadow of
Paul and John.

Ric said his solo career
since his death in 2019
was not catching on
this side of paradise.

So the two dragged their amps
Gibsons and Rickenbackers
and jammed until their guitars
gently wept.

One evening John Bonham
staggered in through the out door
a little drunk and looking for
some band mates.

He liked what he heard
and hadn't picked up the sticks
since his wild days with
Plant and Page.

Over time, the Beetle Cars
featuring Bonzo on drums
slowly climbed the charts
like a stairway in heaven.

Art Attack

The piece breathed the artist's rage at me
all her self-defeating demons screaming at once
echoing lamentations that nearly killed the work
accusations defending her twisted beliefs
murmurs coursing from head to heart
that she will never be what she really could
yet here she hangs in Chicago in living color.

The oils spread flat on a bed of cloth
rise to their intended denotation, taking form,
giving life and breath to both their creator
and all who sink in the vastness of its depths
changing their lives in small, significant ways
shining proof that the artist had no right
treating herself the way she did.

By Pedal

Summer to us latchkey kids
was a ticket to see our city
an open-ended passport

We had Stingrays and Huffys
and hand-me-down custom jobbers
to carry us to the urban edge

On banana seats with sissy bars
hand brakes for sophisticates and rich kids
pedal brakes for the reckless and unwashed

I took pride in pimping my ride
with headlight, speedometer
and one of those geeky hedge flags

Our points of interest were many
Como Zoo, the Mississippi River
or as far as our legs gave us

Today my bike has sixteen speeds
light and speedy with disc brakes
it cost as much as a used car back then

And like that bike from the '70s
it still carries me to new places
freely in the wind and sun of summer

Who I Am

I am an egg in an ovary. I am a glint in my father's eye. I am one of seven children. I am not quite one year-old and suddenly, one of six children. I am too young to realize this. I am almost five and suddenly fatherless. I am sad and completely unaware of the implications that my father's absence will have in my life. I am a student at St. Luke's grade school. I am a defensive end on the football team. I am a bench warmer. I am a cadet at an all-male military high school. I am suddenly obsessed with meeting a girl. I am a B average student with a bright future. I am a stepson. I am a Freshman at the University of Minnesota. I am on academic probation. I am determined to turn my grades around. I am a Geography major. I am a Gopher alumnus! I am a gainfully employed cartographer mapping my future. I am suddenly laid off. I am a borderline depressed unemployment statistic. I am determined to find another job in mapping. I am forced to move to Wisconsin to find it. I am suddenly a Cheesehead. I am a Packer fan convert. I am finally able to know how it feels to win a Super Bowl. I am a pen pal to a woman in New York. I am her long-distance lover. I am her husband. I am the happiest I've ever been. I am a suburban Milwaukee homeowner. I am father to a beautiful girl. I am overwhelmed with both love and new-found responsibility. I am father to a handsome boy. I am tired all the time. I am certainly not worthy of all I have. I am a Systems Analyst in county government. I am suddenly one of five children. I am a man prone to crying because of this development. I am a published author! I am a poet laureate! I am still a horrible golfer. I am suddenly 60 years old. I am closer to death than birth. I am approaching retirement. I am not one to look back but am fully cognizant of the privilege I have had to be part of this beautiful world. I am eternally grateful. I am living life with increased urgency. I am going to tell everyone I know that I love them. I am tired of writing about who I am. I am sorry for the repetitive nature of this poem. I am going to stop now.

The Book of Her

is a thick tome
with three lifetimes
stuffed into one volume.
It has handsome princes
majestic lakeside vistas
trauma, hurt and healing
and that is only chapter one.
The story is set in an
enchanted frozen region
of ice and snow
and despite some distant journeys
that include swimming
with ocean stingrays
and camping in remote woodlands
despite all of that
she chose to live out her days
in the enchanted land of ice;
but not for the love of it
rather because her family lived there.
The supporting characters in her story
are too numerous to count.
and begin with her seven children,
then, in-step another eight
then, in-laws and outlaws
countless friends, family
and partners in crime
—you know who you are.
The story winds through tragedy
bends its way around hope
and is carried by her strong faith.
The morals within are many;
Family always comes first.
It's okay to laugh at yourself.

But most of all,
life is hard, but it all works out . . .
eventually.
Of course, the story ends
as all our stories will
and though we cannot change that
her message was a lesson
in writing a book
that will not soon be forgotten.

Each a Breed of Their Own

Lance was a chewer
shoes, furniture, even Halloween pumpkins

Pepper was a runner
last seen on a dead run down Lexington Parkway

Pumpkin was a lover
a family favorite killed by a car

Brandy was a biter
the ultimate source of her demise

Boris was a charmer
loveable with legs too short for his body

Hans and Franz were barkers
doorbells and knocking pumped them up

Buck was a hunter
a faithful companion in the field

Andre was flamboyant
a drag-queen poodle with a perfect cut

Bentley was a licker
with sloppy kisses, wanted or not

Salten was a humper
with a one-track mind

Spike was a snuggler
quick to your lap, quicker to sleep

Toby was a Terrier
our loyal friend, gone, but never forgotten

These are some of the dogs I've known
with personalities all their own

Funeral Wish

At my funeral
I want you to put on the
J Geils Band vinyl 33 RPM
Blow Your Face Out
and dance until you're
sweated through
because when it
comes down to it
life ain't nothin'
but a house party.
That's my dying request.
And, if instead
you play *On Eagles Wings*
I will rise from the casket
and smash that record
like the woman
in It's a Wonderful Life
because I don't want to
be raised up like a raptor
I want to cut a rug
until I hurt.

2050 Anticipated Trends

(Taken from the 2050 Old Pharmers Almanac)

Glaciation will see a 5% increase due to the reversal of global warming. Polar bears will rejoice. Permafrost will return to an isolated small region in the Arctic Circle.

The floating plastic trash island in the Pacific will become so big and dense it will support a population of 300 people.

Seventeen new antibiotic resistant bacterial strains are expected to come to light.

The new iPhone version 23 will replace most of your friends.

AI solar-powered companion dogs will discover how to run away from home. Forever. Followed by doing it.

An agricultural combine that fuels itself from its own harvest while it drives will be developed that can harvest 40 acres in a single pass to net 33 gallons of ethanol.

Due to steadily decreasing attention spans, all new books will be less than thirty pages long. Poetry will be limited to haikus.

A new species of hydroponic corn will produce an even less nutritious, but significantly cheaper form of high fructose corn syrup.

The Mason Dixon line will be reestablished as a political boundary. It will feature two affiliations, one governing the United States of the North and the other governing the Divided Collective of Unified but Separate Land Areas of the South.

COVID-49 will be a virus that causes an uncontrollable nose itch. Kleenex shortages expected.

All the mature trees previously planted to sequester carbon will become the source of massive wildfires, resulting in record carbon levels in the air and across now treeless plains.

Ocean water desalinization will create mountains of salt significantly increasing the unbuildable land mass of California which can only mean one thing. War.

Haikus for the Loner

social outsider
he's not a fan of small talk
he's deeper than that

she's an introvert
your party—she will not go
it's not personal

he's not a loner
he just doesn't like people
for more than an hour

Minnesota Boys

He left Minnesota
just like me
to find a place
just outside of Delacroix.
Growing up I had
his poster on my wall
a shaggy vagabond
Live at Budokan.
It was included with the LP
and reminded me
there was a life beyond—
beyond the Iron Range
far from 10,000 lakes
somewhere along Highway 61,
maybe all along the watchtower
or just west of Desolation Row.
When I was in college
in our common home state
he was chugging through
his Jesus stage
like a slow train coming
and the critics were not having it
they beat the Jesus out of him.
But he's still touring at 81
picked up a Nobel along the way
and true to his word
he ain't gonna work
on Maggie's Farm no more.

Losing Arguments

The bingo hall was packed
with smokers and blue hairs trying their luck
using wild-haired trolls, plastic unicorns, rabbits' feet
four-leaf clovers, bells, and lucky ducks
at the top of each card channeling winning calls.
Who am I to argue with witchcraft used for personal gain?

She kept her crystals safely stored
in a dark velvet bag with drawstrings
only pulling them out for two purposes
one for luck, the other to "charge" them
on windowsills under the light of a full moon.
Who am I to argue with the forces of geology and lunar energy?

His car had a small plastic statue
of Saint Christopher on the dashboard
the patron saint of safe travels
it was there when he inherited the car from his aunt
he kept it there because he was too afraid to move it.
Who was he to argue safety with a dead saint?

These totems are used to energize the inert
to bring luck, fortune, and goodwill to everyday people
with an estimated success rate of 50/50
users would say it gives them hope, or an edge
others would laugh and say it's all hogwash.
Who am I to argue with either side?

Superior Sister

As a Minnesota boy growing up
all I knew was Superior
with its cold, unforgiving depths
and the lore of its shipwreck song.
To me, it seemed an endless inland sea
with an unknowable, distant shore.
There could not be anything like it,
or so I thought.
Until I met her little sister, Michigan
after a move to Milwaukee in the '80s.
She was equally impressive
-not inferior to Superior-
slightly better behaved, but still capable
of taking ships for her own songs.
She has a warmth not known to Superior
and while not as deep, is still far from shallow
as the middle child in a family of Greats
she is approachable but still demands respect.
She is more Suzanne Vega than Lady Gaga.
She is the girl next door, but don't mess with her.
She is our Superior sister.

Photo Retention

When looking for something else
I discover some pictures
stashed deep in a drawer
smashed together in albums
tattered from neglect.

Apparently portraits of relatives
I was too young to ever know
they wear cat-eye glasses
and pressed shirts
neck ties and print dresses,
fashions of the day.

What am I to do with them
that does not negate their lives
of beauty and richness
or sadness and tragedy
to say nothing of all of
those moments forever lost
outside of the camera's eye?

Though I never spoke
to these black and white relatives,
couldn't name most of them,
barely even knew we were related
it feels inherently wrong to trash a relative.

Instead I am reduced to
forcing them to continue their silence
in a book of yesterday's dreams
a catalog of lives come and gone
squarely summarized in sepia
in volumes with thin white borders.

About the Author

Jim has four published memoirs, *At the Lake, Cretin Boy, The Portland House,* and *Dirty Shirt.* Jim also has five published poetry collections, *Thoughts from a Line at the DMV* (Kelsay Books, 2018), *Genetically Speaking, Reciting from Memory* (eBook), *Written Life,* and *On a Road.* His nonfiction stories have been published in *The Sun Magazine, Main Street Rag, Story News,* and others. His poetry has been featured in *Rosebud Magazine, Wisconsin People and Ideas, Blue Heron Review,* and many others. Jim was the 2018–2019 poet laureate for the Village of Wales, Wisconsin. He is semi-retired and lives with his wife, Donna, in Waukesha, Wisconsin.

www.ingramcontent.com/pod-product-compliance
Lightning Source LLC
Chambersburg PA
CBHW071012160426
43193CB00012B/2015